A spell of

Peter Jay Shippy

saturnalia books

Distributed by University Press of New England
Hanover and London

Saturnalia Books
105 Woodside Rd.
Ardmore, PA 19003
info@saturnaliabooks.com

ISBN: 978-0-9833686-8-7
Library of Congress Control Number: 2013947564

Book Design by Saturnalia Books
Printing by The Prolific Printing Group, Canada

Cover Art: Slow Ending by Yosuke Yamaguche

Author Photo: KBKO

Distributed by:
University Press of New England
1 Court Street
Lebanon, NH 03766
800-421-1561

I would like to thank the editors of the following publications, in which poems in this book first appeared: *B O D Y, The Burnside Review, Connotation Press: An Online Artifact, Crazyhorse, Denver Quarterly, DMQ Review, Fogged Clarity, Guernica, Harvard Review, IN QUIRE, Inter/rupture, New World Writing, Pool, Printer's Devil Review,* and *Zoland's Poetry Annual.*

Table of Contents

for Beatrix & Stella

Untrimm'd

When the great waters left, the sky took the place
    of the sea.

Beautiful as we go

My father spent the period between Elvis
leaving the army and The Beatles arriving

in America painting flowers, striped specimens,
dusk stars, satellites bouncing whammy, stems

refracted through the translucent petals
of a trembling blue harebell, yes, I was born

ravishing an indigo vase, mood iodine,
which way up was not trivial geography

for a boy gleaming like a pot of peach stones
boiling in bootblack, I used my syringe

as a spyglass to record imaginary freighters
oozing over a green brook in the woods

where we lived, nowhere in sight, but knowing
that my work with the invisible, my loneliness

was as sacred as his errant brushstrokes hinting
at water, mossy rocks, fall wind, chapped lips,

I rescued fly mummies from the spider's mandala,
my shadow shadowed minnows, please believe

that the chromium paste spread over my face
gave me the power over wonder's compunction,

while I noted ship movements he combed miniver
off blackberry thorns for his brushes, in sunlight

snapdragons tasted helpless, like soft butter,
epinephrine to me, the cropped figure

of a trembling blue harebell, yes, I was born
oozing over a green brook, in the woods

in America, painting flowers, striped specimens,
ravishing an indigo vase, mood iodine,

at home father rolled his muller over clay
letting his cigarette ash fall in the umber

as the madder cooked, as I danced to the radio,
Sérgio Mendez & Brasil '66.

Morning over coffee and pain au chocolat

When we were young I fell into your ear, we told time
by the rustle of calendar pages turning

across the Zenith's screen, a candle's narrow light
could set our bare limbs to feather, I recall

the commotion of your prayer beads tightening
around my balls, how did we ever grow so unalike,

we kept the magpies up all night for fear we'd steal
their song, you worked in the village library

where my favorite books were banned, I drove
the yellow bus past the stop where you waited

under a cherry tree abloom with plastic bags
from the nearby liquor store, those sweet nods

could set our bare limbs to feather, I recall
your red straw hat, your dragonfly pin, your way

of scolding the wind that hid your hoe in dust,
your mother's lung, dead on her chest, required you

to fill your house in wasp nests so even our breath
stirred their paper seeds, staying up all night

made us appreciate that what was important
was not us, bony people, bleats and pleas, telltales

could set our bare limbs to feather, I recall
the way you moistened my lips with a gin-sopped sponge

affixed to a long stick, now a wooden top
spinning across my desk passes for passion, please

if you see a petition for a lost parrot,
a wayward crow, a magpie gone to air, stapled

to a telephone pole, remember me, still driving
the yellow bus past the stop where you waited.

Eclipses

Nana slapped a phony Fabergé egg
with a black boa and my mother was born

filling the kitchen with the smell of first snow,
Grampus slipped out the window and raced

a greyhound to the coast, on the shelf, a jar
of white rice shook itself silly, like stoned lice,

I was there, her daughter, sipping sack, a witness,
don't ask how or I'll tell you how and then…

there's no going back, in fact, it was me who wrapped
her own bawling mother in the Gazette while

Uncle Maxim greased his balancing pole and split
his pants for work, I read the funnies, specially

the strips with animals that wouldn't exist
when I was a girl, I loved the one with Bugg,

a mustachioed cockroach from Bohemia
who broke English into confetti when he professed

his love for Clarice, a beetle from Rio
with question marks on her wing covers, so

we daubed-on whiteface and donned smoked glasses,
Nana latched the baby to her breast and ordered

a dozen long-stemmed American Beauties
and used the box to construct a pinhole projector,

at first light we were off to watch the cortege
carry the body of Atlas, our strongman,

to his resting place on the spinning stool
at the end of the bar, we rode the boneshakers

to the river and skipped stones at kids until
they handed over their lunch pails, her pupils

were black as pips, snake-eyes, the dog throw,
my mother's eyes struck my eyes like matchsticks,

the sun whistled white as bone, Uncle Maxim
dipped a Kaiser roll into the warm water

then molded it into a dummy and plugged
my mother's red yawp, years later, he would lead

a crack camouflage unit during the war,
they managed to conceal hundreds of clouds

from enemy zeppelins, years later
Grampus's shadow came home and stained the carpet,

years later Nana stuck me to her old tit
and taught me to steer robotic mitts with my thoughts,

years later Bugg's moustache grew into two queries,
as my mother grew older she stopped stomping

the floor like Trotsky, the amazing counting horse,
and so the circus ran away from her,

don't ask how or I'll tell you how and then...
I was there, her daughter, sipping sack, a witness,

Nana slapped a phony Fabergé egg
filling the kitchen with the smell of first snow.

And he makes his hand into a soft gun

I met you on a red day, a day that grew fins
at noon and swam toward the horizon, the moon

and one splintered star, the next day was blue
with tusks and furrowed skin so I rode the bus

to the market to listen to the man who reads
the dictionary to the birds, in rain or sun,

at dusk I phoned you and the day turned *glabrous*,
we went to a movie on a green day, a day

as opalescent as litchi, a movie about a man
without paper who ties his son to a kite frame,

their kite is barred from the great contest, but
his son discovers a passage to Indiana,

on a yellow day we hiked over the ghost
of a tallgrass prairie, waded a stream, climbed

a hillock and spread out a pony blanket
to watch the day migrate north for autumn,

you trained an orange day to spin a web
so we could lose ourselves in perilous orbits,

we made love on a black day, a day specked
with whooping children, hooded and masked, bursting

through school doors, skipping and firing
their Uzis and Colts into the sweet spring air,

I've quarantined our last kiss, we kissed last
at night on a day that clutched a bouquet

of heat-seeking violets to its chest, at dawn
you sang the mysteries through the beads of my spine,

the day you left was white and the white day's
white eyes swam to opposite sides of the planet

on an indigo day, a day that wore a red nose,
I stayed at home to implore my house to grow

a day with a small door, a door the size
of a day helplessly bent to hold us tight.

The moon is the same moon above you

In a snowy meadow Dumbo watches his daughter fall
back to the earth flapping her arms and legs

then rise to reflect her fletching, her angel
is left to sleep while the Dumbos fly home

to their business, a defunct ski lodge, home
for hot cocoa and sake and the soothing sounds

of the Tzarra Twins, the lounge act, Rickenbacker
& Theremin, Satie and Debussy, one of the sisters

is his daughter's mother but he's never sure
which one, from a distance, he's never sure until

they pick up their instruments which one will
set the air on ice, Dumbo sets his flugel

on the rosewood bar, he can smell monsoons,
gooseberry, mango, he blows a little Dizzy,

"A Night in Tunisia" and looks in the mirror
on the wall behind the counter at his daughter

or her angel, raised from the meadow, reading
the 1828 *Webster's* in the lodgerless lounge,

Sushi Chef tucks her red hair under her slouchy
and quarters shiitake with her slicer,

how will I make my trunk meet my tail, Dumbo growls
setting the air on ice, he blows until he's dizzy

on the rosewood bar, he can smell monsoons
tinkling the ivory, Satie and Debussy

on the hi-fi in Bombay, as a boy, as
his parents danced, hindered only by long tubes

from the oxygen tank hooked up to his father
because of a trunk condition caused by years

of breathing nights in Tunisia, they tangoed
across their kitchen, Sushi Chef frowns,

she detests Dumbo's chalky tears, his self-
pity, his inability to forget, to let go

so she stops whetting her cleavers and fixes
two chopsticks under her top lip and barks

like a bull walrus until Dumbo smiles back
into the world where his daughter's mother

karate chops an air where his daughter recites:
hopple, to bind the feet to prevent leaping,

as in: to hopple that unruly wild-boy, Dumbo
digs a tempura cocoon from the snack bowl,

cracks it open and a dahlia-winged monarch
emerges hovering near his ear and scats over

the bridge, the Twins, until Sushi Chef uses
her #3 cleaver to split the butterfly

into the world where his daughter's mother
karate chops an air where his daughter recites:

scat, to sprinkle syllables loosely about, as in:
let the hours scat and fly in endless joy and love,

and Sushi Chef wraps each insect half in nori
for Dumbo and his daughter, his fletching,

the ski lodge's round windows grow fuzzy, like
an iceboat in a crème de menthe bottle

on the rosewood bar, he can smell monsoons
from the oxygen tank hooked up to his father

as a boy, breathing "Nights in Tunisia,"
as his parents tangoed across their kitchen.

Blue, stumbling buzz

Jan van Eyck painted spider webs in heaven,
makes you wonder, mother said, *about the price*

of tea in Bruges, there's a small room, a closet
really, in the Youngstown Free Library

where mother shelved, where she curated masterpieces,
that week, early Netherlandish, outside

it was snowing aurochs and grazers, infrared
pictographs of her face would have shown pentimenti-

of-the-soul, her library was blocks away
from the Niagara, from Canada, what little town

by river, her books were naughty, unspooling
microfiche and running away for weeks at a time,

during her Romanian Dada exhibition
a set of Britannica's committed collage

and self-adhered to a bathroom wall, van Eyck
liked to wear a scarlet turban, after his death

his heirs unwound his head and found a tapestry,
really, in the Youngstown Free Library,

depicting ice skaters on a frozen canal
raving at the feast of the Falling Asleep of Mary,

we took turns licking a Bosch, yellow ocher,
Carmine Lake with a goose egg binder, Baltic oak,

the ashes of my father, her lover, were kept
in a vial hidden in a hollowed out copy

of *The Illustrated Joy of Sex*, so he'd be there
when you needed him, the blizzard had emptied

the building so we closed up shop and slid
on our bellies to The Stone Jug for deglazing,

drinking Genny Creams with cognac depth charges,
we live by drowning for we are people born

from the Niagara, what little town by river,
every winter, hundreds of years ago, the cataract

would freeze, completely, and a carnival was held
below the precipice on the river's apron

with horse-driven Ferris wheels and carousels,
acrobats, dancers, contortionists, bear tamers,

and a steam-driven roller coaster that melted
the ice causing a floe to break away and float

downriver, carrying the Eiswein-sipping tent,
by the time the oenophiles sobered, they could see

Lake Ontario, so they jumped and swam and lived
and where they shored they founded Youngstown,

makes you wonder, mother said, *about the price*
of The Illustrated Joy of Sex, so he'd be there

in a vial hidden in a hollowed out copy
of the soul, her library was blocks away,

Carmine Lake with a goose egg binder, Baltic oak,
my tabard was trimmed in brown fur, boxing hare,

her dress' ornate dagging and under-wiring
made her appear to be pregnant with me

drinking Genny Creams with cognac depth charges,
raving at the feast of the Falling Asleep of Mary,

Jan van Eyck painted spider webs in heaven
where mother shelved, where she curated masterpieces.

Ou es-tu, mon amour

As for me, I became the knife that pares notes
from the sparrow's throat, I flew the fighter

that dropped the bomb on the Cathedral
of Erotic Mystery, as for me, I filleted

your piano, looking for the harp concealed
under the fallboard, then I did what singers do

in arias, I joined the Royal Navy,
Dogsbody, 4th class, mother gave me a bag

of pease pudding, an ampoule of opium,
and a chintz cape slash shroud lined with glitter,

as for me, I was in the kitchen baking
lavender cakes, hoping to snare the honeybees

that dropped the bomb on the Cathedral
under the fallboard, then I did what singers do

in a sacred chantey, I tied my leg
to a rocket and launched myself from the beach

into the sky so I could watch the villagers
race from their high pastures to the sea to grab

their harpoons and set off on their jet-skis
in pursuit of whales, as for me, I spent weeks

with my nose glued to your apse, in my green
mantilla and thong, filling evidence bags

with Meissen dildos, snail shell prayer beads,
tibias and fibulas and leaves of ashen psalm,

as for me, back in real time, without you,
I was coding my way to the monkey house

on easy street, I was shooting H-O-R-S-E
with myself when we smelled burnt sugar, skin,

a plume of brown smoke blocking the sun,
gulls circled, meowing like a sack of children,

as for me, I'm the sentry of a green motel,
over the ancient inland sea, guarding the window

of Erotic Mystery, as for me, I fillet
the salt glazed glass by my teeth and nails,

etching in your eyes your hair your legs your breasts,
tibias and fibulas and leaves of ashen psalm.

Academy fight song

Her mother was a butcher with leopard prints
from cheek to jowl, her mother's knife was clouded

with goose down, her father was a flightless bird,
a looking glass, a 2-way mirror, prison ink,

a masked tomcat in the butcher's window
displaying a ballet of plump hams, her brother

was the maid in the hotel's powder room, handy
with a trowel or a straw, her brother was in leaf,

her sister was a grey room, an intestine,
a rustling under your boot, her sister, Miss

Fisheye and her brother Mr. Clammy Cellar,
the butcher's knife shone like hare tracks in snow,

she was a virgin and a swan song, which meant
mojo juju, which meant that every flautist

in XYZville was hot for her corpse
so they could sculpt her immaculate bones

into instruments with the facility to summon
spirits and demons, poignant and pleased, her father

was a gizzard stone, a rusty dawn, a sailor's
warning, her mother's window was lit with leis

of sausage, boar and meadow buck, her black eyes
sparkled in oyster shells on my paper plate

on a park bench near the fishmonger's shack,
her father was the knife in your underwear

but not the butcher's knife, nope, her mother
the masked tomcat in the butcher's window

clouded with hyena spots from tongue to toe
from brow to ovary, from calf to steak,

her sister, her brother, sold her out, her father
sold her to a bag of smoke, a man who was a sack

of rank cash, a scalpel, a musician with fat lips
so she ran, she was the woman running through

the park where I collect trash, who fell heels
over head, I pulled a glass shard from her bare foot

and I looked into the mirror's splinter and saw
the butcher, her mother, her mother, the knife

clouded with goose down flying at three throats
filling her window with sweetmeats for Easter,

I kept this vision to myself, I watched her rise
and run along the red wall, into the old forest.

The engineer of moonlight

The scar on her left breast was Utica,
her lips were Dar es Salaam, cold springs

in Duluth caused that cough, like a cat hawking
songbirds, babblers and warblers, the crow's feet

under her eyes were a walk-up in Iowa City
where we heard Schumann's "Child Falling Asleep"

on a baby monitor, it struck us as sunken
music, the orchestra going down with the ship,

women and children first, the bruise on her hip
was bottle green from her bedroom wall, well,

who hasn't pursued the slow disco, the keen scar
on her right knee was skating rinks in July,

her hair, her mother's and her mother's hair
was New Bedford, Lisbon, chestnut, planted near

her mosaic in the tea garden because they say
hair keeps haints away, her strong legs were nights

swimming the ancient inland sea, from Appalachia
to Laramidia, her smile was très nice,

was Nice, where a plummet from a bicycle left her
with a gap between her front teeth, between

the genuine and the acrylic, her wooden leg
was Sears Roebuck, 1867, she kept it

on the mantle next to a picture of her 4 greats
grandmother who lost a limb on a battlefield

in parts unknown, a family secret, she said,
one she never told for fear it might explain

her skull's camber, which was smelled like Fez,
so unlike Assam's liaison with the curl

of her neck, her neck so unlike giraffes or swans,
thank god, outside of a poem who wants to be

inside a simile equation with a zoo,
her desk was apple, barn wood, the family farm

where hers picked sugar beets for years after
they arrived from Beets, thus her purple hands,

her records were from 1963, Memphis and Seoul,
her voice was Little Łódź in South Buffalo,

listening to her sing "Blue Monday" made me
nostalgic for the distant future, her tears

were products of the Argentine, her tears
were Cedar Rapids General, the NICU,

where we heard Schumann's "Child Falling Asleep"
on a baby monitor, it struck us as sunken

music, the orchestra going down with the ship,
women and children first, the bruise on her hip,

her skin was quick, wolf moonlight on a loco-
motive driven by a sleeping engineer.

Kinderspiel

Before we boarded the black train father buried
our bobbed tails and showed us how to pull pink skin

over our long ears, the countryside streamed over
our compartment window, green and thick like tongues

swollen with honey, warm beer, clover and thorns,
the taste of summer fevers, winter ague, at dawn

conductors brought eReaders, chrysanthemums, and tea,
to wile away the days father committed us to

a dictionary letter, I had K, from Ka to Kyrie,
we spread my mother's scruffy sheepskin coat

on the floor for exercises, heels turned out, chins
joined, busts advanced, mouths shut, sister pruned

my bandages, trimming bark from the hound,
when the ink monitor distributed blues

we used pens made from straws and hat pins to draw
portraits of our fellow passengers that we sold

for red cents, I wonder if they knew, in 4th class,
a man taught me to play duck on a rock with cubes

of Merck cocaine and his daughter's diaphragm,
I spent my days in the train's cinema studying

the lovers, how lips and mouths purl, once after
digestifs father gave his wingtips to the porter,

in exchange the man fastened us to the roof
with duct tape so we could watch the cosmos

katzenjammer like a killcow dancing the kazachoc
and dodge the train's next stop, Frontier Station,

checkpoints, and magicians looking to buy specimens
for red cents, I wonder if they knew, in 4th class

and if they knew why didn't they ring the bells,
use their boots tipped in long knives, hang our pelts

from the flag-pole and collect the gilt, the pelf,
before we boarded the black train father buried

everything except for the clothes on our backs
and a book of moths, emeralds, scarlet puffs, pink

fringes, sea spots, greens from altogether elsewhere,
moths like this no longer exist, father answered,

*after the bombings and flattenings they transformed
into ash clouds, Cinderellas, smut, dust, ash*

professors, our little masters of camouflage, still
I recall the vase of souring mums, dissents, red

as rabbit giggle, tendons, hearts, grass-stuffed guts
and those in 4th class who gave me a way to live,

to wile away the days father committed us to
fringes, sea-spots, greens from altogether elsewhere,

the taste of summer fevers, winter ague, at dawn
scowling with sunlight, until one day it was the day

we arrived, *walk straight, father said, proud, bear
your fangs and levitate at the drop of a top hat.*

The strangers

for David Daniel

Mother died today or was it yesterday,
I can't quite remember, is funny unless

it's your mother and she died intestate
in flagrante delicto under me, under

the influence in a state not Nevada,
so cut the gas track and laugh the engine,

we have a paper jet to fold, next arrest
the Mink Fez in Memphis, Tennessee, let's sit

in a pleather booth with the reddest ribs,
the friskiest whiskey, and our universal baby

monitor, punching its buttons and bending
antennae until we hear "Green Onions"

putting some soulful grub to sleep, *Let's funk,*
you'll say and I'll acquiesce, I'll press

your gloved hand between my paws as we float
toward the ceiling where a bare bulb buds

frayed wires, black threads off a defunct web,
Cowboy, pitch your tent, you'll say, reacting

to my reaction to your foot in my mouth,
your mouth against my zipper, as a podiatrist

you're a brilliant psychiatrist but before
I can spill my bean we'll feel the soft cuff

of butterfly nets against our heads as the staff
pulls us down from our hairy aerie so

I can't quite remember is funny unless
Mother died today or was it yesterday?

Twisted

The birthday party was evaporating, the cake,
crumbs, the donkey, pinned, Mary-the-boy-pony

was being loaded into his trailer for the ride
to his next gig at the teen orphanage, the clown

was sitting on a picnic bench, sipping bubbly,
free-styling for the die-hards, preaching to the kids

about cinema and quantum mechanics, *there's a scene*
the clown said, as he twisted blue balloons

into a giant squid evading Japanese fishing nets
but awakening Godzilla, a scene in The Red Balloon

where our hero, Pascal, walks le ballon rouge
across a bridge as a train passes underneath

filling the shot with steam, white smoke, poof smoke,
a scene that moves backward and forward through

the history of film, foremost and first
it's an echo, a riff, a bald-faced homage to

L'arrivée d'un train en gare de la Ciotat,
The Lumière Brothers tour de force, the clown said,

as he twisted black and white balloons into a lamb
whose eye was the eye Luis Buñuel slices open

with a razor in *Un Chien Andalou* and the lamb
David Lynch used as a baby in *Eraserhead, legend*

has it that the opening night crowd, which included
Sigmund Freud, Fanny Cerrito, and Alfred Jarry

was so frightened of the image of a life-sized train
steaming toward them that people screamed and ran

to the back of the theater, the clown said, twisting
olive, sienna, cerulean and flesh balloons

into "Study for the Nurse in Battleship Potemkin,"
a painting by Francis Bacon based on the mouth

of the screaming nurse in the Odessa sequence
in Eisenstein's film, *it's the scene, Pascal*

on the bridge with his balloon lost in the smoke
that Spielberg presses into Schindler's List

as the girl in the red coat, the clown said, twisting
glow-sticks and white balloons into the bone slash

orbiting nuclear weapons satellite
from *2001, Spielberg knew that our brains,*

those conflating machines would fold the girl's coat
into the boy's balloon so we would hear the train

filling the shot with steam, white smoke, poof smoke,
a scene that moves backward and forward through

the chuffing death camp trains spewing their fogs,
the clown said, twisting red Technicolor balloons

into the red shoes from *The Red Shoes, Spielberg knew*
Le Ballon rouge w*as about Christ, but not the Son*

of God Christ, no, just the Jesus who's a Jew,
any questions, the clown asked the remaining child,

can you make a dog, the boy asked, *let me tell you*
about Tarkovsky and Andrei Rublev, the clown said,

pulling a pack of balloons from his floppy shoe
thinking, Toto or Precious, Asta or Laika?

Black

Let's begin with the black rain gutters berried
and snailed, a box that stows black lips, keys

that made his tin robot spark, wings witching
the fishing boat, the landscapes in your arms

as you did it, wings of insects paddling
our hair where the forest wolfs stars,

your father's pea coat, sweet cigars, slippers,
the black lips blooming on Christ's face

in a Presbyterian church, Lake Ontario, nail
polish extending through the aquarium,

alder bark, the frozen path between orchards
and vineyards with quick black grapes

geared up for sweet wine, brain meat, an iris
in the taxidermist's kit, russets, wet kohl,

a kite tail snapping over our heads on a hill
where we stood watching the ferry deliver hours

to us, hairy baseballs, in the beginning,
winter flies confessing under the window grille,

quarry talus, salamander, tallgrass, sweet water,
bee smoke, zero, the whorl of an ear, lamb crimps,

a feather in her special hat high on a shelf
between a jar of teeth and a jar of nickels,

a clutch of burnt fur on a bumper, clubs, spades,
braids of fog, flesh, blood, blood, November

sunbeams, plum juice, the velvet-lined box
you inherited from your grandmother, train tracks

lush with knotweed and paintbrush, patience,
a sharp pencil skating over vanilla vellum,

your father's pea coat, cigars, the slippers
you inherited from your grandmother, train tracks

in your hair where the forest wolfs stars,
alder bark, the frozen path between orchards.

Brontosaurs

After the massacre the soldiers filled
their victim's ventilated skulls with seeds,

they hung red poppies and clover from trees
and lampposts, all over the city, the countryside,

letting the wind cyclotron the buzz, once a year
on a snowy evening the village collected

their hopeless utensils, bent forks, rusted spoons,
knives past smartening and put them into a capsule

topping a pillar of antique Saturn rockets
and launched the package at the stars, that is,

they fired it toward us, we prefer to believe
this was their way of showing their love, their wild

gesticulations were a ballet, probably,
and their catchy epithets were just lyrics.

A romantic age

From our window the only signs we saw
were in Japanese, morning snow, I guessed, falling

on winter willows or kitchen utensils, cheap,
she cleaned her spit valve and scratched crooked licks

into her stave pad with a yellow nubby,
a library pencil, my contrabassoonist

composed in a hum thick with Honshu bamboo
soaked in Limoncello, on the plaster mantel

was an ultrasound of her, inside her mother, womb
spume, slug, clapper, ship in a bottle, sloe plum

listening for wind, her river, its golden reeds,
from our window the only signs we saw

were kids loading their snowballs with sharp stones
as their tongues invented new words for winter,

when my contrabassoonist played she arched her back
and a skin of music covered my eyes, her notes

were in Japanese, morning snow, I guessed, falling
into her stave pad with a yellow nubby,

when I was a boy I was put behind the piano
for talking during class and refusing to duck

and cover, years passed until I was discovered
by a tuner who taught me to feed on vibrations,

we met when she came into my shop, hoping
I could cure her instrument's whooping trills

and a skin of music covered my eyes, her notes
spilling from our tub, over its claws onto

the cold floor, it was nice, for us, to jump
like hares, hopscotching toward those sharp stones,

our souls, hidden in the cast iron radiator,
spume, slug, clapper, ship in a bottle, sloe plum,

when my contrabassoonist played, she arched her back
raising her belly and breasts out of the water

spilling from our tub over its claws onto
the peeling parquet tiles and our thick shadows,

I balanced our snowball on her navel and we fucked
until the ice revealed its grief, such small seeds,

she fell asleep with my ear to her chest, her lungs,
listening for wind, her river, its golden reeds.

Wine, honey, flowers, night, etc.

Shunned sleep, all night, listened to the pea
under my daughter's pillow trying to hear

her voice below the telecaster, the moon scribbled
my face with silver and kohl, near dawn I fell

from bed and scratched my bean against the floor
to light my aura, made my bare feet squeal peeling

over the icy floorboards through my empty shotgun
into the kitchenette to microwave day old coffee,

I opened the window and peed on the dandelions,
the pigsweed, the thistle, the creeping Charlie

and I saw the pale horse, or was it a mule, eating
apples from a collapsing tree, once upon

when I had a family we'd ride the train
to the country and stare at cows, sheep and grids

of golden wheat, once upon we paid a farmer to let us
pick his pears, was it even legal to ride a horse

in the city, or was it a mule, a white donkey,
when the animal turned to drink skunk water

from the deflated kiddie pool I saw ten
red digits painted on her side, I gave my neighbor

the finger, zippered-up, and found my cell
and started dialing, her long mane was braided

with gold, velvet ribbons that flickered under
branches of maple, red and sugar, a soft breeze

pushed the chains on my porch that once upon supported
an oak glider, the hinnie, or was it a pony, leaped

my hedges and cantered down the sidewalk, I chanted
and sang and beat my palms against the drywall,

the pigsweed, the thistle, the creeping Charlie,
her voice below the telecaster, the moon scribbled

rooms as I tried to recall that phone number,
if that's what it was and if that's what it was

I knew I needed to call upon that tremolo,
I grabbed my daughter's pink, 3-speed Stingray

from under the porch and peeled out to chase
apples from a collapsing tree, once upon.

Anthology

A mouth sings ballads, a mouth sucks a lemon,
a mouth hides uncouth words under its tongue,

once a month a mouth opens wide to let
moonlight strike its pigheaded lungs, a mouth

flutters during the movie's scary part, the part
where a mouth opens the heavy door and takes it

on the chin, when a mouth whistles "Misty"
a cab appears to drive a mouth to the sea

where a mouth lures a pearl by screwing up,
by puckering like a lonesome oyster, a mouth

swells in the spring to keep from blowing away
the names of the flowers, a mouth presses against

the door, like a dog, like a dog's mouth waiting
for the squall to end, a mouth fills with water

to score the ball lightning, a mouth needs
a mouthful of ash to knead into a ball, cheek

to cheek and once across the teeth until a world
is ready for the oven, a mouth swallows

the cake, the saw, the salt lick, a mouth swallows
a golden swallow and flies for the storm's eye,

to stop its mind from blowing steam a mouth ties
its tongue into a fist, to raise a new clapper

a mouth grows a ruby cocoon from its gums,
even crows cry when a mouth fills with brown leaves

and curdled apples, a mouth must inhale a ton
of sulfur to blow just one halo, a mouth chews

on its spectacles and sighs, someone enters
through the eyes to take the mouth by surprise

and together they eat the candle flame, a mouth
soothes a stone to fashion a whisper, a blush streak,

a mouth wakes up late at night aching for milk,
for mother's nipple, when a mouth finds another

mouth they form a little spindle to weave a woof
for the devil, to keep Mr. Scratch at bay,

sometimes a mouth hides, a mouth hides under a veil,
a mask, a smile, under starblink, a prayer,

a mouth hides under wax lips until it tries
to kiss the sun and is revealed, burnt and sere,

a mouth applies a balm of snowflakes, a mouth
raises its meat slipper, a pink flag, no surrender.

4 a.m.

When I woke, The Palace was empty, the house lights
were up and the movie screen was white as a blackboard

hidden under the proof for a difficult problem,
someone had written a number on a yellow post-it,

seventeen was stuck to my jacket, the smell
of oil and butter made my tongue work a kernel

from between my teeth, a kernel is an atom stripped
of electrons, no music, just the wet hiss

of the steam organ's brass pipes catching its breath
in the film, the heroine was constructing

a palace of toothpicks, but her work was threatened
by her paramour's music, his trumpet's mute

(hidden under the proof for a difficult problem)
made her parapets tremble, a mute swan throbs

its wings in flight to signal the lamentation,
I heard their Cubans spearing the parquet floor

before I saw them tango up the aisle, a stout man
and a reedy redhead, their cyclonic dancing

made the velvet curtain ripple like a sail
snapping at the Westerlies, I recognized her

from the ticket booth and him from concessions,
seventeen was stuck to my jacket, the smell

of the steam organ's brass pipes catching its breath,
shedding its skin as one dancer dipped the other

in the film, she hung her stockings on the line
across an alley, between apartment buildings,

letting them fill with rainwater, for her moat
she carved a squadron of wooden ducks, I think

it was counting those decoys that put me to sleep,
when I woke, The Palace was empty, the house lights

made the velvet curtain ripple like a sail
of electrons, no music, just the wet hiss

snapping at the Westerlies, I recognized her,
enjoy the dénouement, she asked, *quite moving, I lied,*

may I cut in, I asked, *seventeen*, she replied,
anyway, it's time I did the books, the man offered

his hand, I led, I led his head to my shoulder,
his hair smelled like lamb's lettuce and capers,

he whispered, *before the heroine boarded
the airship she said "I am incapable*

of making palaces that do not contain my love,"
we moved our lips to the song in her heart,

I sank into his crush brilliantine waves, lush
as blue medicine, the gas flame that calls my moth.

10 haiku & 1 epithalamion

They say they found me in frozen foods, stretched out
in the cephalopod case rowing the air,

praising the canned corn moon, as a boy I hung
from a cherry limb listening to ballgames

on grandpa's transistor, a blonde spider,
grief skin, *lieben*, sunlit orb weaver quitting

amen corners to run over wallpaper, a left hand
crawling through Ravel, hunting for missing limbs,

a breast in my cell phone's screen, my eyes climbed
from her nipple to a wrist, an arm, her face

and I rose with her body to exit the Kiang train
at the wrong station, after the martini shot

my cinematographer blew ballads along
a grasshopper thong that made our sweet crew weep,

in a dim bar I drank beer and gazed at a pig
somehow deflating, in a jar of brine, when we met

I was too shy to speak so I wrote a note
and placed it with a caterpillar in a bottle

thrown into the ocean for an octopus
to find and open and raise the chrysalis,

the butterfly, to the spring air to lick her ear:
put on your clothes, the producer said to the cast,

we're shutting down, kaput, closing shop, kaput,
after my wife's death-complying flight

from the cannon barrel into the lion's mouth
the clown car arrived at our front door

and they rolled out, with floppy shoes and red dicks
for noses, with sprays of squirting flowers,

I fell asheep counting fools, they rolled out
too broken to sleep, I steered the bus around

the rotary and Keanu cradled me
in his arms, little suns took our measurements.

When the boys were so pretty

A small apartment, the window faced the station,
autumn was leaking over the train tracks,

he sat on the couch staring at his reflection
in a teaspoon, she stood at a table, her back

to him, furiously polishing spoons, melon spoons,
soup spoons, salt spoons, apostle spoons, ear spoons,

in the kitchen a tea pot whistled for its tongue,
the wind shook the house, looking for nesting hair,

the floor between them was steeped in frayed wires,
vacuum tubes, wooden knobs, and horn speakers somehow

playing the glad rags' rag, after the song faded
he said, *Who's there, Who's there*, she echoed,

the teaspoon jerked free of his hand, it rose
and hovered inches from his grasp then ascended

and disappeared, he stood on the couch, looking up,
waving his arms until he too, levitated

and vanished, she continued to polish mote spoons,
coffee spoons, ash spoons, love spoons, marrow spoons,

autumn was leaking over the train tracks,
the wind shook the house, looking for nesting hair,

the winter sun, like a brass button, trickled
into a box of photos in the corner of the room,

when the doorbell rang, she stopped to answer,
he entered and walked right through her to retake

his position, she grabbed a lead jelly spoon
from her table and wrapped his hand around it

so he could stare at his reflection, her back
to him, furiously polishing spoons, cheese spoons

absinthe spoons, egg spoons, sugar spoons, sporks,
a small apartment, the window faced the station

where customers were jumping from the platform
into a pile of radiant leaves, orange and red

vacuum tubes, wooden knobs, and horn speakers, somehow
in the kitchen a teapot whistled for its tongue.

Among my swan

I prefer praying in the neap dark, with lilac
backlighting, playing the glockenspiel or shaker,

chanting through a vocoder, never setting
my syllables on the firmament, I stitch myself

into sharkskin, toss rock salt into the air
and catch it under my tongue, I prefer sitting

on a chintzy carpet in a room struck dumb
in the Hotel Buffalo, hard boiling one egg

in white wine, in a tin pot, on a hot plate,
watching that red hieroglyph bleach the bird

into a yellow bloom, pluck, my soul revs
as I conduct the service elevator

to the siren's basement, I jimmy open
the window and abscond, dear, Lord, I lickety-

split to the pig Latin district, hopscotching
to the hard currency bars to lead the chorus

in psalms as heavy as warrants, knuckles aging
in formaldehyde, I prefer hanging onto

the strap as the trolley takes my sweet life
for a turn along the sea, a virtuoso plays

a little serenade on her virtual keyboard
and God appears, pluck, his cigar box uke

sends spines down our shivers, the dogfish blues,
we watch ourselves rumba in God's pearl nose stud,

chanting through a vocoder, never setting
in formaldehyde, I prefer hanging onto

a couple kissing at the Tiki Hut, her hand
stretching across his chest so I can lick her ring,

I walk along the strand, enjoying the people
plumping in the sun, dinner rolls rising,

the sea foams and spumes, a sleeping pill in a cup
of dentures, olé, my mouthful of dreams, olé.

Lope de Shakespeare Vega

for Bill Knott

I needed snow to kill the darkness and darkness
to make the snow which left me with a fsh

skating laps on a pool of vichyssoise, parsley
and water chestnuts, garlic and minced onions,

I spent my days in a floating chaise, smoking
myself into a doughnut over the former pleasures

of her body in my bed, her thick red hair
booed my white sheets as we perpetuated

the American songbook, I was a man with needles
and fishing line which led to steady work

down at the hockey rink mending split lips
for the baby Sabres which led to quilt circles,

used vinyl, and heroin, scars like the signatures
of the illiterate, garlic and minced onions,

when I'm cooking, she said, butt out, one misstep
can change a recipe into an autopsy, parsley

and fishing hooks, in the stereoscopic photo
on my parent's mantle I'm wearing a veil

and her wedding dress in the tundra at dusk,
loving cups, glass globes filled with used rice, white

vinyl spinning the kingdom of the blind
where the one-eyed man knows what he's missing,

you can't have his body until the spring thaw
my family told the linesmen, I spent my days

smoking myself into a doughnut over the time
she used silver duct tape to bind me to her

chest and hiked 10 miles from our single-wide
on the shore of Lake Ontario to Niagara Falls,

to the train station to strew Bengal rose petals
at the *20th Century Limited*

carrying Jorge Luis Borges from Boston
to Buffalo for a lecture, the argentine

Argentine, after the express passed, hundreds
of aficionados swept-up the flowers,

walked to the cataract and threw them over
the American falls, that night we joined an armada

of tractor inner tubes, floating the river,
the lower Niagara, singing rounds

of "Rainy Day Women #12 & 35," we beached
yards from our home where we spent our days

skating laps on a pool of vichyssoise, petals
booed my white sheets as we perpetuated

used vinyl and heroin, scars like the signatures
making the snow which left me with a fsh,

I looked up at the blades skating figure eights
and rang the Pachelbel, she lowered her coaster,

I held a rainbow trout wrapped in funny pages,
what do you call a fish without eyes: fsh,

and I took my place in the car, on Comet,
on Cyclone, on Phantom, on Viper, on Thunderbolt.

Ringaround arosie

We bent the Bug's backseat, sipping iced green tea
and vodka, have mercy, I toasted, deploying

the plastic test strips from a pregnancy kit
as swizzle sticks, my drink was positively not

heavy with child so I nibbled red nail polish
from Eva's long toe, her eyelids shuddered

like a spray of angelica, a bouquet fit for
a glassed queen, no one would choose to live like us

except me, the shopping cart cowboy smoked stinkers
as he wrangled and screamed obsequies

into his earpiece, the pick-up next to us
was cutting coupons and nodding, with alacrity,

to hair metal, I put an ice cube down my pants
to arrest my stiff kitten, so as not

to appear craven, no one would choose to live
here where winds dance our shirtsleeves to dust,

the parking lot was quiet as dawn, although
it was dusk, the pharmacist who was so kind, stood

between a Mustang ragtop and a mini van
in the doughnut shop's drive-through line, texting,

she had told us about a gold farming factory
in Manchuria, where teenaged workers

killed video monsters and harvested treasure
that was sold on eBay to Japanese students,

a factory that suddenly became infected
by a torch song that spread from screen to screen

like a virus about unrequited love
that made workers too sad to kill ogres,

the police made the pop singer record a new tune
about blissful love, and the spell was broken,

and ogres were once again slain with impunity,
So the moral is, she said, as she rang up Popov,

gum, and First Response, *beware false positives*,
the name on her employee badge was Ginger Hu,

the plastic test strips from a pregnancy kit
like a spray of angelica, a bouquet fit for

a glassed queen, no one would choose to live like us
like a virus about unrequited love,

it was dusk, the pharmacist who was so kind, stood
in the doughnut shop's drive through line, texting.

Horticulture

I propped my skateboard against the bars of the cage
and watched the tulips bend toward oblique light,

milky glass, conch, mouths, rabbit ears, listening
to planets turning grist, on a wintry morning

I propped my skateboard against the bars of the cage,
April something, according to the gospels

people who stare at flowers make our Lord sad,
Christ will turn you into a toad or an old man

wearing a crushed mitre, a mushroom, your trousers
stuffed with a squirting flower, asleep on the train,

near the menagerie a man was setting-up his cart,
herbs, blue cabbage, tomatoes, and bell peppers,

it was their obstinacies that made me lean
toward the huddle, shaven flesh, their humming,

sometimes you hear people sing, *I don't want to live
like a parasite*, I want to make my own way

like a widow, my body covered with mud, wearing
veils woven from the sweetest grasses, my hair

fired with tulips and I'll dance wild and corrupt,
sometimes you hear people sing, I don't want to live

toward the huddle, shaven flesh, their humming,
near the rose pens a woman skewered her sausages

with popsicle sticks, she dipped them in corn batter
and baptized them in chubby, hissing oil,.

a high fog pretended to be the sky, a guard
put a finger to his nose, we had a moment, so

I retreated, I placed my board under my arm
and walked away, thought of our mother, lying

on the green sofa with her book of crosswords,
with her bare, clever tail, I bought her a pepper

and thought of the traces of the time when plants
were birds, with feathers and three small sharp teeth,

when plants were a delicate fish tail in limestone
on the green sofa with her book of crosswords,

I rode to work as the morning bells rang away
April something, according to the gospels.

The passenger

I feel fractious, high mutt, a problem
· that figures blackboards into chalk clouds, cirrus

shit, let me show you my tap-dancing scar, cheek
to scowl from performing wicked scissor kicks

across Moscow's notorious ear-waxed floors
as a boy, night after night, two shows on Sunday,

I never wore shoes, no, those were for firebirds,
instead I used a nail gun to shoot steel brads

through my feet, I was thrilling in my pashmina
leaving the boards crossed with my ruby score,

now I ride a trolley to work, one circle pit
after the next, at Back Bay the doors open,

now I surf the crowd, aiming for the exit,
seizing hair extensions and cauliflower ears

for balance, my fog-laden Alps are bereft
of Romantics, as you carry me toward the hole

in the car, to my calcite station, I can smell
the gladioli incense, the pumpkin ales,

hummingbirds are stripping coconut from munchkins,
through the terminal's skylight I see orange cranes

lifting girders, building a nest, lift me
toward the milky rift, let me show you my wallet,

genuine tongue, serious giraffe, money talks
blue streaks, please lick my myrtle scented pits,

please kiss my Goddamn Florsheims, as a boy
I never wore shoes, no, those were for firebirds,

now I surf the crowd, aiming for the exit
seizing breast implants and penile extensions

for balance, my sun-smacked deserts are bereft
of pilgrims, as you carry me toward the tumulus

I can taste pretzels and honeycomb, the glow
from your laptops tuckers out, I can almost taste

the bronze escalator, I can hear a teenager
wearing 20-hole cherry Docs and a Baby Bjorn

play "Immigrant Song" on her cello,
I'm a little ship on your waves, hauling me

to market, strew my hair plugs with mistletoe,
and strangle me with ruby laces, please.

My mother's last word, an apprehension

One meaning is laughing academy dropout,
another is to squander an inheritance

chasing mutant butterflies in Fukushima
with Chou Chou, a strung out chaologist,

searching for the sound of one wing clapping,
when verbed it articulates the rapport between

a Shaker rocking chair and a hickory floor,
when screamed in a coup d'état it implies that

your mother will wear my mother's army boots,
rogue ethnolinguists traced its sprout

to a palimpsest in a john at a Shell Station
ten miles south of Eulogy, Texas, but

in Iowa it describes a carny divorce,
seven spins around the carousel, backwards,

one summer farmers in Alberta found the unit
cut into their durum, in a steamer trunk

under my bed is a Polaroid of my mother
on a rocky beach somewhere in Sweden,

sticking out her tongue at the photographer,
at 23, after giving birth to me

she'll whisper my name into her doctor's ear
and die, in the pine-oak forests of Mexico,

etymologists believe that Mescalero shamans
used peyote to gently coax its fundamentals

from their lowing intestines, Maria Callas,
in her unpublished autobiography,

recalls using a broken hockey stick
to etch that word, an Italian epithet,

into wet cement near the old Met, wrecked
in '67, what was it that sad old beast said

about Noah's ark of syllables, *iamb*
by iamb, when written in classical Sanskrit

it coveys the smell of *rosewood soaked in monsoons*,
I read my mother's last word first in a balloon

above my Nana's head as she hummed a song
about lambs, sun bears, and the Vietcong.

The echoing cliffs of Kaibito

The class discovered the bodies on a field trip
to a tall grass meadow on a bluff above the sea

as they gathered pollen, hazelnut and dandelion,
for their school musical, *Orpheus Descending*,

arriving at the scene the police took photos
of the exposed ribs, *like oak, like a catboat's*

said the detective, scribbling calculations
on yellow post-its that she stuck to her black Mac,

a specialist in sacred geometry, she measured
the chains of thyme cinching sachets of molars,

the teacher encouraged his students to move
at the same beat and shout bad names at the corpses

as they gathered pollen, hazelnut and dandelion,
for the last act, the passage to the fugitive kind,

frozen to death, in a snowy field, decades ago
said the detective, scribbling calculations,

the class Punchinello used his trick cane to point
at a snail as it advanced across a tibia,

*our government has trained gastropods to sniff out
the cancers of gastronomists*, he said, rainclouds

like rayographs, tarsals and cuneiforms, slid
away, out to sea, the class clapped for a fireboat

blowing its horn, the detective placed her nose near
the foot bones, gilt-edged, *like polished pear wood,*

suicide through the ingestion, the detective said,
of potassium cyanide, commonly used

by the Victorians to retouch photographs,
pigeons into angels, three-headed dogs

for the last act, the passage to the fugitive kind,
when pollen would be sprinkled over the dancers

to evoke an opium dream, the cane grew a bouquet
that squirted water into the boy's white face,

Hades hunts poets for our delicious eyes, plucked
by talons, dried, ground, rolled, and smoked, he sang,

for their school musical, *Orpheus Descending,*
arriving at the scene the police took photos

of the pebbled beach and the Sisters of the Chapel
of the Star of Sea, *L'Étoile de mer,* blessing

pods and schools, offering rice cakes, chanting
for the whales and dolphins to return to the land,

under a blue sky seamheads played catch with a ball
& socket joint, a girl, the teacher's pet, threw signs

at a snail as it advanced across a tibia
blowing its horn, the detective placed her nose near

the napping Punch, *boy funk and chinaberry,*
a string of greasy mussel shells hung from his ears,

what do you hear, she whispered, a whirlybird
carrying the forensic team broke the calm

for the last act, the passage to the fugitive kind,
under a blue sky seamheads played catch with a ball.

Last requests

Draw a zigzag moustache below my nose
in permanent ink, stain my lips with black cherries,

carve a horn from my sacrum and blow *my baby there*
so cold so sweet so fair, take my eyeteeth

from round her neck and plant them in the orchard,
use darning needles and fishing line to sew

my palms together, distribute my ribs
to the old-timers at the pound, fill my navel

with vitamin water, lily pads, false grunions
and meditate on me, as my dispensation

to the divas of Icelandic synth pop, skin
my soles, craft a tom-tom, and transmit my pulse

to Reykjavik, bleach my mandible and nail it
above the old barn door, plop my balls

into a jar of salt water behind the bar
on the top shelf of the lower depths, plug the dam

with my thumb, use my pubic hairs to flower
a few bald Barbies and gift them to the daughters

of your enemies, use my spine to measure
the first blizzard of the season, my tongue

shouldn't be blamed for a lifetime of broadcasting
bullshit so please, friend, scrape mine osculator,

mine canticle, mine chatterling, my taste bulb
and return her to her tribe at the bottom

of the sea, ride your bike to the arboretum
on a perfect day in October and give

my ears to that 1-legged keytarist, maybe
he can pass them off as black truffles, use my

vertebrae for Scrabble tiles and my skull to drive
the nail that held my picture into your wall,

take the beeswax from my ears so I can hear
one damned song, but fill my mouth with nectar

so that honeybees will love me at last
(*saw my baby there so cold so sweet so fair*)

pack my eyes into my heart, you know why,
and at the end of night, make of me a kite,

use my humeri as frames and dried sweetmeat
as paper so that I may sail toward the sun,

a rōnin seeking an end to dissonance,
trying to discover harmony and long tail.

Ruined and disused dance halls,
The Bhūta Ballroom, Lockport, NY

Moths ham up the rafters, the applewood purrs.

Also Available from saturnalia books:

Each Chartered Street by Sebastian Agudelo

No Object by Natalie Shapero

Nowhere Fast by William Kulik

Arco Iris by Sarah Vap

The Girls of Peculiar by Catherine Pierce

Xing by Debora Kuan

Other Romes by Derek Mong

Faulkner's Rosary by Sarah Vap

Gurlesque: the new grrly, grotesque, burlesque poetics edited by Lara Glenum and Arielle Greenberg

Tsim Tsum by Sabrina Orah Mark

Hush Sessions by Kristi Maxwell

Days of Unwilling by Cal Bedient

Letters to Poets: Conversations about Poetics, Politics, and Community edited by Jennifer Firestone and Dana Teen Lomax

Artist/Poet Collaboration Series:
Velleity's Shade by Star Black / Artwork by Bill Knott
Polytheogamy by Timothy Liu / Artwork by Greg Drasler
Midnights by Jane Miller / Artwork by Beverly Pepper
Stigmata Errata Etcetera by Bill Knott / Artwork by Star Black
Ing Grish by John Yau / Artwork by Thomas Nozkowski
Blackboards by Tomaz Salamun / Artwork by Metka Krasovec

Winners of the Saturnalia Books Poetry Prize:

Thieves in the Afterlife by Kendra DeColo
Lullaby (with Exit Sign) by Hadara Bar-Nadav
My Scarlet Ways by Tanya Larkin
The Little Office of the Immaculate Conception by Martha Silano
Personification by Margaret Ronda
To the Bone by Sebastian Agudelo
Famous Last Words by Catherine Pierce
Dummy Fire by Sarah Vap
Correspondence by Kathleen Graber
The Babies by Sabrina Orah Mark

A spell of songs was printed using the font Adobe Garamond Pro.

www.saturnaliabooks.org